Mindful Moments

Mindful Moments

Living Your Best Life
In Imperfect Times

Eric Vance Walton

Mindful Moments
Living Your Best Life In Imperfect Times

First Edition

Copyright © 2020 by Eric Vance Walton

ISBN: 9798576093182

Cover and book designed by Lubosh Cech *artbyluce.com*
Cover photo by Greg Rakozy *unsplash.com*
Illustrations by Ophelia Fu.

To order additional copies of this book please visit Amazon.com

I dedicate this book to my father, Verlo Victor Walton, the man who taught me how to be a man. Someone who's gone through unspeakable challenges in his life and survived with kindness still intact. Thank you for everything you've done for me. I will always remember our time together and how much fun we've had.

Contents

A Just Pause

Standing here
on the precipice
of nowhere
in particular,

Feeling open,
ready
for whatever's next.

Paying attention
to nothing
but my breath.

Expectations
of anyone nor
anything seem
desperately naive.

Understanding,
the true nature
of how
lucky I am
to perceive
such beauty
and bliss.

My soul
is strong
and these shoes
are still comfortable
because I've
taken millions
of humbling steps.

A Note From the Author

I can remember this one particular moment in time like it was yesterday. It was a clear, crisp winter night and I must've been nine or ten years old. I was all alone and lost in thought, as I often was, looking up at the pitch black, star-filled sky feeling perfectly at peace. I stood there for a long time contemplating how incredibly vast the universe was.

In that moment it dawned on me how much our universe looked like the human brain under an electron microscope. Then I thought, *Could our universe, in fact, be a huge brain? Are we existing, on some microscopic level in that incomprehensibly enormous brain? This led me to yet another thought, Do we have an entire universe inside of our own brains?*

Over the past few decades I've invested countless hours both learning about and training my own mind through meditation. During that time I've learned a few things about how this universe inside of myself works and also the ways in which it connects to and works in conjunction with the larger universe we all exist in.

I'll tell you the most valuable lesson I've learned. You'll never permanently increase your quality of life by – focusing solely on making money, adding influential people to your network, acquiring more stuff, or by trying to impress or please those people around you.

If you want to dramatically change your life for the better you must turn the searchlight of your attention inward. You must make it your life's mission to work on and gain a greater understanding of yourself. Once you do this, you begin to understand the profound interconnectedness of your physical existence, your quality of life will improve in a lasting and dramatic way, and you'll never see your place in this wondrous universe the same way again. This entire world and the people who occupy it provide us with a mirror that allows us to better understand ourselves. All we have to learn to do is pay attention on a deeper level. It's my wish that *Mindful Moments* helps to show you how to do that.

No matter how bleak things might seem, substantial change can begin to happen in the blink of an eye and it's never too late. The only way we will change this world is by changing one person at a time. This transformation starts with you.

Prologue

Most of us, at some time in our lives, have experienced a moment of almost perfect peace. It's in these moments we temporarily lose ourselves. It's as though we're wrapped in a cocoon of pure joy and contentment. These feelings can be triggered while experiencing a golden sunset, the warm glow of a campfire on a crisp night, or our children happily at play. I call these mindful moments and they're so profound that it's difficult to describe in words how good, content, and whole they make us feel. However, these mindful moments are usually fragile, short-lived, and evaporate in a few seconds.

What if there was a way to train your mind to experience more of these moments? What if, with practice, you could begin to string these mindful moments together until you begin to exist in this place of joy, peace, and contentment more often than not? The key to experiencing this next-level quality of life is by mastering the art of living mindfully.

Learning to live in a state of mindfulness is easier to learn than you think, it requires nothing more than a subtle shift in mindset. This book will teach you simple techniques that will allow you to live your best life and be the best version of yourself despite the challenges and negative circumstances unfolding around you.

At the end of most chapters in this book is a section dedicated to meditation as well as blank journaling pages for you to jot down thoughts and ideas. The meditation exercises are very simple, by design. This *5, 5, 7 meditation technique* has been honed over twenty years of practice and designed to be easy to remember and effortless to apply. You'll be able to test out the concepts presented in each chapter and use the book to chronicle your personal journey to living a more mindful life. If you're reading the eBook version on a mobile phone or tablet simply place your finger on the Notes page and "long press" your screen to activate the Notes feature in the Kindle app. Use this notes feature to document your observations and results.

Note: *For best results I suggest reading only one chapter per week and practicing that chapter's meditation section at least once a day over the course of that week while utilizing the journaling (Notes) section of that chapter.* After you're through with all ten chapters, if you feel the need to reread the book, please do so. I also recommend keeping the book and revisiting your journaling sections when you're feeling emotionally depleted or challenged in any way. I'm a firm believer that the best way to change the world is to never stop working on ourselves. I hope you find this book to be useful in the journey to becoming the absolute best version of yourself.

Chapter One

Media Detox

Our perception of the world today is clouded and skewed. For the sake of survival, through countless centuries of human evolution, our brains have been hardwired to give priority to certain things or situations that could pose a threat to our well-being. Our ancient ancestors evolved to notice threats and negativity first. In their world this paid off in a huge way. The ones who spotted those dangerous predators lurking in the shadows first lived to see another day and propagate our species. Today, by comparison, the kinds of dangerous predators they encountered are nearly non-existent but the residual propensity in our DNA to search for and focus on the negativity and perceived threats is still there.

The mainstream and social media have found very effective ways to exploit this negative bias encoded deeply in our DNA. For decades, the mainstream media has become more effective at triggering our negative biases, controlling us through our own emotions of fear and hate for higher network ratings and increased online clicks. More recently social media platforms have taken this emotional manipulation to a dangerously epic extreme. These social media platforms' algorithms are hacking our brains without us even being conscious of it, getting us addicted to them, and then selling our attention to the highest bidders.

The result of this extremely dangerous business strategy of the traditional mainstream media, big tech, and social media companies is the absolute polarization of society that we see today. If you want to learn about precisely how these companies are eroding the fabric of our society I highly recommend watching two Netflix documentaries, *Social Dilemma* and *The Great Hack*.

Negativity paired with ideological polarization driven by the media is our world's true epidemic and it's set us on a path of destruction. Sadly, our society is increasingly losing sight of the wonderful thing called consensus; being able to see valid points in opposing views. I say sadly because the middle of the road is often where the real truth lies. This magical balancing point between the two extremes is also where the larger problems of humanity get solved. By losing sight of this we're missing out on countless opportunities to learn, to teach, and to evolve further as a species.

"See if you can catch yourself complaining, in either speech or thought, about a situation you find yourself in, what other people do or say, your surroundings, your life situation, even the weather. To complain is always non acceptance of what is. It invariably carries an unconscious negative charge. When you complain, you make yourself into a victim. When you speak out, you are in your power. So change the situation by taking action or by speaking out if necessary or possible; leave the situation or accept it. All else is madness." – *Eckhart Tolle*

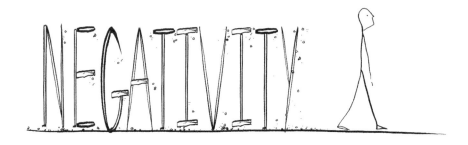

It's sometimes difficult to remember that if you live in any first world nation today you, statistically, live in the safest and most peaceful era in history. It doesn't seem that way because the lens of our perception is distorted by the barrage of negative news. Today there's a growing undercurrent of fear and hatred, an epidemic of doom and gloom, a cacophony of dysfunctional and toxic voices on social and mainstream media outlets. Worst of all even friends and family are turning their backs on one another due to differences in opinion. All of this emotional manipulation forces us into an unhealthy and toxic state of being and greatly diminishes the quality of our lives.

Disharmony has become the norm, so much so that it's very difficult to find a way out of the mindset it induces. *What is the best antidote to the twin poisons of negative bias and emotional manipulation?* Although It's impossible to escape all sources of negativity how you choose to focus your attention is still well within your control. The single best antidote to this toxic state of being I've found is a complete and total media detox. Do your best not to consume any mainstream news for three entire days. Also, log off of any social media for that same amount of time.

This seventy-two hour day detox will give your mind and body a chance to renew and cleanse itself. The lens of your perception will begin to be wiped clean and you'll start to discover your true self again. If you're diligent, you'll begin to notice a shift in mindset after just the first day. The new positive emotional state you'll gain will become every bit as addictive as the negative bias. If followed with discipline, this three day media detox will begin a positive feedback loop that will become an incubator for the birth of a new state of mindfulness in you. You may even find that you want to extend it for a longer period of time.

As we age we realize how precious time is and our lives are too important to allow ourselves to be controlled by anyone or anything. Remember, every minute wasted on hate and negativity is a portion of our lives lost. When we begin to consciously reclaim our lives, minute-by-minute, we also begin to take back both our freedom and power.

Your life is like a garden. Negativity and emotional manipulation are two of the most invasive weeds in that garden. They'll choke out all that's good in your life, if you let them. You must weed your garden on a regular basis. This awareness and practice will set the stage for a very powerful form of self-directed evolution that will change the course of your life in wonderful and unimaginable ways. Don't waste one more second of your life immersed in negativity. Seize control at this very moment. Begin to notice the good, the beautiful, and the abundance that surrounds you and you will attract much more of it into your life.

"Nothing you have today will last forever. Not your job, your house, or your car. Not the people who are closest to you. Not even the people who vowed to never leave your side. Take a moment and accept the fact that life is short and you don't have a lot of time to be with your loved ones. Someday all those people will no longer be around you, and you can't possibly know when. Cherish them while you can." – *Mai Pham*

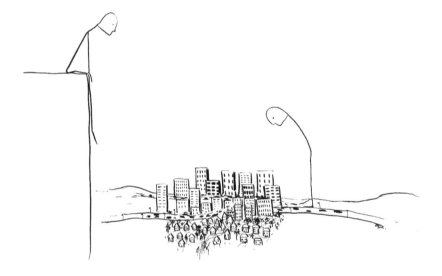

Use the *Notes* section at the end of this chapter to jot down a few words about your experiences every day of your seventy-two hour media detox. Before putting pen to paper contemplate things like – *Are my mood, mindset, and worldview changing? How do I feel differently? Can I see others' point of view more clearly? Am I communicating with others in a different way? Is my anxiety, and/or anger levels changing? Do I feel more rested when I wake up in the morning?*

It's not very often that an author will tell you not to read any more chapters of their book but this is precisely what I'm asking you to do at this time. For this chapter to be as effective as possible I will ask you not to read any further until you've completed this three day period of media detoxification and journaling. On the fourth day read through your notes and analyze the progress of your transformation. When it's over you should be much more conscious of the quality of media you consume and the many ways in which it negatively changes you. Once you're conscious of how these media platforms influence you, the power is in your hands to purposely decide how you want to reintroduce them into your life.

NOTES

NOTES

NOTES

NOTES

NOTES

Chapter Two

Fear and Worry

W hen I was in my late teens and early twenties I feared almost everything and my life was small because of it. It took me years of struggle and countless self-help books to begin to feel better, but I found this only offered a temporary solution. I continued my search for something that would allow me to heal and regain a semblance of balance in my life until I found the only thing that really helped in a lasting way, meditation.

I often wonder what my life would be like today if I hadn't begun practicing meditation. More likely than not I'd still be shying away from the things that frightened me or made me feel uncomfortable. I would have continued traveling down the path of least resistance. I'd probably still be working the same warehouse job I started after high school, or something similar, and daydreaming about what it would be like to be a writer.

The company I worked for never hesitated to remind us that we were expendable and paid us just enough to keep us there. I drove a forklift and heaved eighty pound boxes onto a conveyor belt for eight to ten hours a day. My writing was limited to whatever spare time I had left, which often was very little. While I was lifting those boxes I would often think about how great it would be to win the lottery and live the life I always imagined. Back then I believed that success was something that randomly bestowed on certain people, if they were lucky, instead of something that you planned for and worked towards.

The problem with the younger me was I far too passive, reactive, and didn't take enough risk. I was letting life events, fears, and those people around me dictate and define what my life should be. Instead, I should have been more proactive and made an actionable plan to begin my own individual journey to success and personal evolution. One day I woke up and realized I was just plain tired of being afraid of everything and living such a small and limited life. I began to stand up to my fears. When I did this I began to realize how incredibly exhilarating and empowering it was to step outside of my comfort zone. Standing up to fear became addictive. Slowly, my small life began to expand and change radically for the better.

"Persist – Don't take no for an answer. If you're happy to sit at your desk and not take risks you'll be sitting there for the next twenty years." – *David Rubenstein*

One of the things I've learned from over two decades of meditation practice is fear and its equally toxic sibling, worry, are one of the biggest roadblocks to living our best life. If left unchallenged, fear continuously stalks us, nagging away deep inside of us. Unless you stand up to fear, each time it defeats you it will grow stronger.

In actuality, *Fear* is - **False Evidence Appearing Real.**

Fear's influence can make us limit our potential by forcing us to live too cautiously and not take enough risk. It extracts us out of the magic of present moment and into the realm of worry. Most of the time our worries and fears are irrational and unfounded but they can feel as real as life and death. Succumbing to these emotions can drastically limit our personal and professional potential and overall quality of life.

The truth is that worry and fear have three things in common. Both of them are bullies, liars, and cowards. Like any bully, they'll gradually loosen their grip on you each time you stand up to them. The opposite holds true as well, each time you give into them they only get stronger and even more oppressive.

"Too many people are thinking of security instead of opportunity. They seem to be more afraid of life than death." — *James F. Byrnes*

We often see successful people and think to ourselves, *If I could only be as fearless as them, life would be easy. I could do anything!* I'll let you in on a little secret, everyone experiences fear; some have just learned to hide it better than others. Always remember, courage isn't being unafraid, courage is feeling afraid and doing it anyway.

If you want to truly change your life start to stand up to your fears. Begin by standing up to the smallest of your fears and build up your tolerance over time. Once you start seeing results, standing up to your fears becomes a very exhilarating obsession.

Success

Both a seeker
and a scarred sage
I am approaching
that certain age
when you
learn that
each decision
matters.

Fear is both
a bully and
a coward
stand up to it
more than
once and it
shatters.

My heart
has felt
the glory
of the dawning

of this dream
to be found
a few steps
beyond the
searing pain
of defeat.

Each time
you fall
you must rise
again
to your feet
because with
persistence
you will win
and this
success is
so sweet.

Meditation

Throughout the course of your day today, pause, and try this simple meditation. Begin by sitting upright in a comfortable chair then:

1. Close your eyes and imagine standing next to the bravest person you can think of. INHALE for a count of 5 (sniff the flower). As you inhale, imagine absorbing some of their courage they radiate inside yourself.
2. HOLD the breath for a count of 5. Feel the thrill and radiance of that courage coursing through your veins and settling in the deepest recesses of yourself;
3. EXHALE for a count of 7 (blow out the candle). During your exhalation imagine your worries and fears escaping through your breath and floating up and away into the sky; and
4. REPEAT for as long as you like (at least 3 repetitions).

Mindfulness Exercise

Now open your eyes. After this pause, take a mental inventory of your worries and fears. Zero in on just one of your persistent fears that you feel limits your potential and quality of life and write that fear down in the *Notes* section at the end of this chapter. Find a way to stand up to this one fear, even if it's in a small way. As you do this, jot down what you did to stand up to the fear and how it made you feel.

Keep chipping away at that same fear, vowing to stand up to it in some way every day for the next five days. If it takes more than five days, that's okay. The important thing is to stay focused on it until you feel that it's sufficiently released its grip on you. Once that first fear is slain and laid to rest, just move onto your next fear, and so on. Be sure to use the *Notes* section at the end of this chapter to chronicle your progress.

Once you begin to systematically stand up to your fears your life will begin to expand and transform in wonderful ways. You will quickly learn that courage is even more contagious than fear, and your newfound courage will inspire others.

NOTES

NOTES

NOTES

NOTES

NOTES

NOTES

Chapter Three

Setting Boundaries

Setting boundaries with yourself and with others is one of the main keys to maintaining happiness and success. This is one of the most profound lessons I've learned; and I'm still actively learning it in middle age.

The first steps to being able to set and enforce proper boundaries are: 1. knowing exactly who you are and what behavior you consider to be acceptable; and 2. realizing your own strengths and self worth. Internalizing, remembering, and most importantly, enforcing boundaries is like having a superpower in life.

The holidays are an opportune time to practice setting boundaries with family. Family gatherings can present the perfect petri dish for dysfunction, every family has their fair share of it. During the holidays people in our social circles often, jokingly, complain about how dysfunctional their families are. As the great Geoffrey Chaucer said, *"...many a true word hath been spoken in jest."* No matter how much work you've done to evolve and heal from the scars of your past, being around people you've grown up with can instantly renew those old insecurities and negative patterns of behavior.

Almost every family has one person, or several, who drinks too much and/ or says or does inappropriate things. These kinds of people thrive on chaos and like nothing more than to antagonize and lure others into arguments. They also have a habit of putting people down to try to make themselves feel better. This is the opportune time to begin to define and enforce your personal boundaries and put an end to unhealthy cycles of behavior. It's okay, and perfectly healthy, to let these people know that the way they're treating you is unacceptable. It's equally as important to remember you have the option of choosing to not engage with them until they acknowledge your wishes and treat you with the respect you deserve.

Setting boundaries is just as important in business as it is in your personal life. To be taken seriously we have to make sure we consistently hold business associates accountable. We do this by making sure they keep their promises, treat us with respect, and calling them out on their bad behavior when they fail to do so. Anything else is like giving these people permission to mistreat you.

Letting those you work with know immediately and diplomatically when they've stepped over the line of what you deem acceptable behavior might be uncomfortable in the short term but they will most often adjust their behavior or move on to a new target. If not, there is little in this life that is worth being mistreated for.

It's also very important to design your own life plan. Define what's most important to your own happiness and well being. If you've never taken the time to design your own life plan, it's never too late to do so. Once your plan is in place, stay tightly focused on those goals and dreams, protect and nurture them as though your life depends on it.

Be wary of anyone who tries to divert you from your own dreams and lure you into assisting them with theirs. Before you agree to any such arrangement make sure that their dreams, personality, and morals are in very close alignment with your own. There are many highly charismatic people out there in the world who will try their best to enlist you to help them with their dreams at the expense of your own. On the outside, these people might appear to be brimming with confidence. Oftentimes, this is a false front and they are secretly insecure about their ability to achieve success on their own.

"If you don't design your own life plan, chances are you'll fall for someone else's plan. And guess what they have planned for you? Not much." – *Jim Rohn*

Through the years I've learned to be very wary of people who are overly charismatic, shower you with shallow and/or insincere flattery, and make lofty promises. In my experience this is usually one the first red flags of people with manipulative, sociopathic, and/or narcissistic tendencies. These kinds of people usually have an established agenda and view other people merely as commodities to extract their wants and needs from. Their goal might be to extract your ideas, gain an introduction to your network of contacts, or coerce you into contributing some kind of financial assistance. One thing is for sure, it's rare that these kinds of people have your best interest in mind.

Often we shy away from calling people out on their bad behavior because we don't want to rock the boat or seem like difficult people ourselves. We feel like we're personally assaulting the one who is treating us badly instead of just communicating our own expectations of what is okay. Ironically, by letting bad behavior slide and dodging confrontation even once we're indirectly giving people the greenlight to mistreat us. By being passive we often set ourselves up for a lifetime of victimhood and loss until we learn our lesson. We can always get a new job, make more money, or meet new friends but the one thing we can't regain in this life is lost time.

Being brutally honest with others isn't really being brutal at all, it's actually being compassionate. When you are *compassionately honest* your life, more often than not, becomes instantly better. Your compassionate honesty also provides those people exhibiting the toxic behavior with a chance to see themselves in a different way. It also provides that person with an opportunity to correct the behavior, if they choose to do so.

> "Compassionate people ask for what they need. They say no when they need to, and they say yes when they mean it. They're compassionate because their boundaries keep them out of resentment." – *Brene Brown*

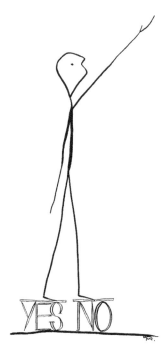

Life becomes so much easier when you learn to communicate your wants, needs, and expectations to those friends, family, and colleagues around you and establish acceptable parameters for behavior. The very first step is knowing who you are and recognizing your own self worth. Then you must demonstrate to the outside world that you know exactly how valuable you are. There's no better way to accomplish this than through the introspection and valuable insight gained in mindfulness and meditation.

Meditation

The 5/5/7 technique of seated meditation allows you to center yourself so let's start with that. Begin by sitting upright in a comfortable chair then:

1. INHALE for a count of 5 (sniff the flower). Imagine a very powerful and positive, golden-colored energy gathering in your body that will protect you from harm and negativity;
2. HOLD the breath for a count of 5. Feel this bright and positive energy radiating within and around you, getting brighter and brighter with each repetition;
3. EXHALE for a count of 7 (blow out the candle). Imagine the positive energy surrounding your entire body like a bright bubble or force-field, protecting you from all of the negative people influences in your environment; and
4. REPEAT for as long as you like (at least 3 repetitions). You can also practice this meditation before situations you know will be challenging or after situations where you've felt particularly vulnerable.

After you practice this very simple meditation technique for even a few minutes it's very helpful to linger in that place of peace and calm, focusing your mind on your self worth and the unique set of skills you bring to the world.

Mindfulness Exercise

Begin to think deeply about designing your own life plan. Use the *Notes* section at the end of this chapter to list out some of your short and long term goals. *What do you really value in life? What are basic wants, needs, and expectations when it comes to interacting with others, both personally and professionally?* Also list a few of your "deal-breakers"; things that you absolutely refuse to put up with. It's very important to physically write these down and keep them in a place that you can refer back to them often so they're kept fresh in your memory.

As you go about your day, begin to identify interactions and situations when you feel your boundaries are being crossed and let people know immediately when they do it. If you do this in a diplomatic way you'll find that most people will honor your wishes. For the few who refuse to honor your boundaries you must be honest with yourself and decide if you're willing to deal with their bad behavior. If the answer is no, you have to be prepared to end that relationship until they're ready to give you the respect you deserve.

Change usually doesn't happen overnight. It takes work to rewire your brain after lifelong patterns of behavior. In the end, the result of setting and enforcing boundaries will be: a higher quality of life; more self-confidence; fewer feelings of resentment; more respect from those around you; and a trustworthy inner circle of friends who you know you can really count on and vice versa.

Remember, say *NO* when you need to and *YES* only when you mean it.

Chapter Four

Self Care

A s we travel down this crazy and unpredictable road of life one of the largest and most deceptive of all the pitfalls we face is losing ourselves. This is especially true for those of us who are givers, by nature. If you're a giver it probably makes you profoundly happy to see those around you happy so givers naturally try to spark those feelings of happiness in others. Givers usually develop a reputation for being stable, empathetic, encouraging, capable, and helpful individuals and because of this they naturally become a support system for friends, relatives, and co-workers.

If you're a giver by nature people will begin to seek out, rely on, and expect this kind of support from you. Many times these people won't, or aren't capable of, providing you the same support in return. Over time, constantly giving and rarely receiving creates an energy deficit within the giver. This situation can quickly spiral out of control and can end up being an unhealthy drain on our time, emotional, and physical wellbeing. If we find ourselves in these unbalanced relationships, it's a good idea to begin to set some healthy boundaries as we touched on in the previous chapter, Setting Boundaries.

"Self-care is so much more than a beauty regimen or an external thing you do. It has to start within your heart to know what you need to navigate your life. A pedicure doesn't last, but meditating every day does." – *Carrie-Anne Moss*

If we're paying attention our minds and our bodies will give us clear signals when we're taking on too much and sinking into that energy-deficit mode. It's very important to be constantly mindful of the signals your mind and body are sending you. The signals can be easy to miss if you're habitually distracted or not paying attention. If you are experiencing brain fog, feeling frazzled, sluggish, and/or irritable for long periods of time, chances are you need to take a pause in your day and recharge. These feelings of depletion are like our soul's "check engine light" coming on and when that happens it's wise to pay attention and make some time for self-care.

You may think taking time for yourself is selfish but it's actually the opposite, it's truly selfless. After all, it's impossible to be the best versions of ourselves and help others when we're constantly feeling physically drained and emotionally overwhelmed.

These moments of self care don't need to be two-week long vacations in the tropics. Ideally, these moments of self care should be like tiny pause buttons in your day for you to press exactly whenever you need them and feel instant relief. They can also be inserted right into a specific part of your daily schedule when you know you feel regularly stressed, like immediately after you get home from work.

"If you feel 'burnout' setting in, if you feel demoralized and exhausted, it is best, for the sake of everyone, to withdraw and restore yourself." – *Dalai Lama*

These pause buttons can be a variety of different things to different people – a secluded reading spot and twenty minutes alone with a good book, a drive in the car alone while listening to the radio, a workout, a walk in the woods, a long soak in a hot bath, a meditation session, or an hour long massage. Moments of self care are anything that gives your mind and body a few moments of pause to replenish, recalibrate, and renew your energy. We all have things that leave us feeling rejuvenated and it's up to you to identify what works best for you. This takes mindfulness.

Using Tech For Wellness

It's very helpful to do a *mindfulness check-in* a few times a day. A simple way to remind yourself to do this is to set a recurring reminder on your mobile device to send you notifications once or twice a day with a messages like:

Is it time to take a PAUSE?

How are you feeling?

or simply,

Take a deep BREATH.

Also, it's imperative to take note of when and how often you're feeling depleted. You may experience low energy levels and feelings of exhaustion once every few days, once a week, or even once every two weeks. Once you've identified your own personal pattern set a recurring notification on your phone with a message to remind you to do something extra special for yourself. Ideally this should be something that allows you to recharge like – time alone, a massage, an hour soak in a hot tub, an extra long walk, whatever activity that helps you restore a proper sense of balance.

Meditation

This guided meditation can help restore and renew you in a very short amount of time. Find a quiet place. Sit upright in a comfortable chair with your eyes closed and concentrate on your breath for a count of thirty before you begin.

1. INHALE for a count of 5 through your nose (sniff the flower). Envision you're breathing in a pure, bright, and healing light that recharges you with energy and vitality;
2. HOLD the breath for a count of 5. Imagine this healing, energizing light spreading throughout your body from the tips of your toes to the top of your head;
3. EXHALE for a count of 7 through your mouth (blow out the candle). Envision the bright light being exhaled and filling the entire room you're in and enveloping you in a blanket of warmth, security, and comfort; and
4. REPEAT for as long as you like (at least 3 repetitions). You can also practice this meditation any time you're feeling emotionally or physically exhausted.

After you practice this very simple meditation technique for even a few minutes it's very helpful to linger in that place of peace and calm, focusing your mind on preserving and radiating the light within you.

Mindfulness Exercise

Now that you're feeling more centered from the meditation above, take five minutes to think about which people, things, or circumstances in your life trigger stress, discomfort, and habitually drain your energy. Also began to think and be more mindful of the times of the day you typically feel the most depleted.

Write all of these things down in the *Notes* section at the end of this chapter. Also, jot down some ideas about how you could re-engineer your life to remove some of these sources of stress to maximize the quality of your existence. Revisit what you've written in the *Notes* section often. Systematically eliminate as many sources of stress as you can so you need to take less and less of these kinds of self-care pauses.

Now contemplate what activities leave you feeling revitalized and refreshed. Use the *Notes* section at the end of this chapter to list five of your favorite methods of mentally and emotionally de-stressing. When you're feeling generally frazzled or life is feeling a bit out of control, practice the meditation above then refer back to this chapter's *Notes* section as a reminder of what you need to do to rejuvenate yourself and regain a feeling of proper balance again.

NOTES

NOTES

NOTES

NOTES

NOTES

NOTES

NOTES

Chapter Five

Listening To Understand

It's perfectly natural for us as humans to want to evolve, to improve our level of happiness, and our quality of life. Most of us are seeking actionable ways to experience a better life while making the very least amount of effort to do so. Listening to understand is one of the most efficient ways I know to begin to experience life on a new level, but it isn't an easy thing to master.

Are you bad at remembering people's names right after you first meet them? I used to be plagued by this. At social gatherings I would constantly have to ask someone else to remind me the name of a person I just met. If you find yourself struggling to remember someone's name after first meeting them it's a very good indicator that you're "listening to reply" instead of "listening to understand." This doesn't necessarily mean you're a bad listener, it could also be an indicator of some level of social anxiety.

"This is the problem with dealing with someone who is actually a good listener. They don't jump in on your sentences, saving you from actually finishing them, or talk over you, allowing what you do manage to get out to be lost or altered in transit. Instead, they wait, so you have to keep going." —*Sarah Dessen,* Just Listen

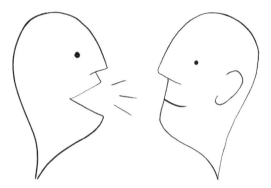

Communication is the foundation in which all human relationships are built. If the person you're speaking with feels they're not being heard then you're not truly connecting with them as well as you could be. In fact, by not fully listening you're doing them, and yourself, a disservice. By not fully listening to the person who is trying to communicate to you you can make them feel slighted and unimportant even if it wasn't your intention to do so. Think of how frustrating it is when you feel the person you're speaking with seems distracted and isn't listening to what you have to say.

In the English language the words "listen" and "silent" contain the exact same letters and I'd like to think this is no coincidence. To listen deeply we must first learn to quiet our minds and set aside our egos. We must fight every urge to jump into a conversation and interrupt them in the middle of their thought-stream. Despite our best intentions, there's rarely good reason to do this.

When socializing, there's no need to prove to anyone how much we know, interrupt to share a similar experience, or try to "one up" an experience they're telling us about. When we're not speaking and someone else is, we have one job and one job alone, that is to simply listen. Being a good listener will leave most people with a much better impression of you than anything else you could say or do to try to impress them.

In social interactions all of us want to be heard but life changes drastically when you begin to truly, Listen to Understand. Not only will those people you're communicating with feel heard, instantly forging a connection with you, but you will gain a much deeper insight into the kind of person they really are.

Deep listening takes practice but once you master it, people will feel a stronger connection with you and vice versa. It will upgrade your personal and professional relationships more than you can even imagine. When you learn how to listen fully and properly you will be able to count yourself among a particularly rare group of human beings. Those people you interact with will feel understood, enriched, and soothed in their interactions with you.

"We have two ears and one mouth and we should use them proportionally."
—Susan Cain, *Quiet: The Power of Introverts in a World That Can't Stop Talking*

Also, you will learn more from listening than you can believe. Most people are truly fascinating in their own unique ways. I like to say, *"All the world's a library, and each person a book."* This universe is trying its best to teach us all of the lessons we're meant to learn. Some of those lessons are being taught through others so it's very important to be present when communicating with them. Each moment of our lives should be spent being fully conscious so we don't miss out on any of those lessons. The way this universe works is if we miss the lesson the first time, it will be repeated. Often the next chance to learn that same lesson is more harsh so we're not as apt to miss it.

Using Tech For Wellness

A good trick I've found to remind myself to listen is to make a custom wallpaper and save it to the lock screen of my phone. We all look at our phones probably a hundred times a day so seeing this word repeatedly will subconsciously burn it into your brain.

If you'd like to try this yourself take a photo of the illustration below and save it to your lock screen or as the custom wallpaper on your mobile phone. Each time you open your phone you'll see it as a reminder to listen deeply when you're communicating with others. Use the *Notes* section at the end of this chapter to jot down the details of your attempts at deep listening and record the results and reactions you notice from others.

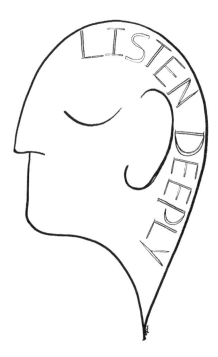

Meditation

This simple meditation will help to solidify the intention of becoming a better listener. Find a quiet place. Sit upright in a comfortable chair with your eyes closed and concentrate on your breath for a count of thirty before you begin.

1. INHALE for a count of 5 through your nose (sniff the flower). Imagine listening to someone. Instead of words, a nutritious and gratifying energy is emanating from them as they speak. You can only absorb this energy while you're listening and not speaking;

2. HOLD the breath for a count of 5. Fully absorb this positive energy and lock it inside of you;

3. EXHALE for a count of 7 through your mouth (blow out the candle). During exhalation, release your urge to speak while others are trying to do the same; and

4. REPEAT for as long as you like (at least 3 repetitions).

Use this chapter's *Notes* section to list details of your interactions within the next week as you become more conscious in your communication with others and begin to listen on a deeper level. *How differently are you beginning to feel as you're listening more deeply? How are other people reacting to your newfound listening skills?*

NOTES

NOTES

NOTES

NOTES

NOTES

NOTES

NOTES

Chapter Six

How You Do Anything
Is How You Do Everything

As I mentioned in the prologue, when I began this book, I decided none of the subjects I would be writing about would be forced. I wanted the topics to naturally bubble up, letting the universe dictate to me the subject matter and timing. One phrase kept popping up into my consciousness, *How You Do Anything Is How You Do Everything*. In the beginning I had no idea where I picked up this phrase or why I kept thinking about it.

After doing a little research I learned that, *"How You Do Anything Is How You Do Everything"*, is actually the title of a self-help book written by author, Cheri Huber in 1998. After some introspection, I realized why I was meant to write about it. In my younger days I was very lazy, impatient, and allowed my life to be ruled by my fears. Like a lot of people out there I almost always took the path of least resistance and then wondered why I never experienced success or substantive change in my life.

Once I fully committed myself to a lifetime of learning the craft of writing it changed everything for me. After years of rejection slips I dug in my heels and vowed to become the best writer I could possibly be. When I did this other areas of my life began to change. I realized the commitment to constant improvement, pride in my craft, and patience gained from writing was naturally spilling over into other areas of my life. Almost three decades later, I know I will never be a perfect writer. However, I can guarantee that if I keep my commitment I'll be better next year than I am today.

In making the commitment to be the best you can be at something you learn volumes about yourself. Writing was just the delivery system of this lesson for me. For you that delivery system might be something entirely different. It could be anything that piques your interest or fills you with positive energy – art, playing a musical instrument, learning a second language, baking bread, a hobby, or renovating a house. It can even be something as simple as properly sweeping the floor.

> **REACH — The past is present in all we are, a living legacy of each joy and sorrow, every struggle and victory, however small and seemingly insignificant. The way we laugh, a certain smile, how we hold our hands or sweep the floor – we are new branches on the same tree of life and this is our time to reach for the sun.**

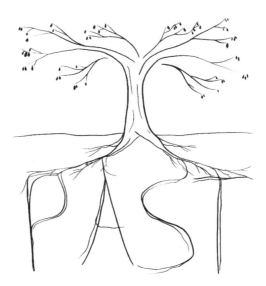

In truth this modern age has showered us with conveniences but has robbed us of many other things that are extremely valuable. One of the things that it has stolen from us is the desire and time to pursue perfection. By constantly being forced to value quantity or output instead of quality we've suffered in ways that we don't often think about. We've also drastically reduced our quality of life and shortened our attention spans in the process.

In today's world there's a high value placed on performing as many tasks as we can possibly do at once. The buzzword is *multitasking* and every prospective employer expects you to mention how great you are at it in your resume and in interviews. Multitasking may increase output but at what expense? While more output may make company owners and shareholders richer on paper it often comes at the expense of our individual inner peace. This frenetic juggling act also is often counter productive and has a negative effect on the quality of goods we produce, and the services we provide.

"Life is a series of moments. The quality of attention and action that we bring to each moment determines the quality of our lives." – *Dan Millma*n

Mindfulness Exercise

Pick one single thing you've always wanted to be better at, it can be anything. Write your choice down in the *Notes* section at the end of this chapter. Make sure it's something that fills you with joy, possibly something from your past that once made you happy.

Now do a deep dive, geek out on it, learn everything you can about that single thing until you become as good at it as you possibly can be. It makes no difference how small of a thing it is you choose. *Why?*

Because the skills you acquire in the pursuit of perfection in any one thing will spill over into the other areas of your life. The feeling of satisfaction you get from realizing you've done your best is both contagious and addictive and it will gradually change your life for the better.

I can tell you that this practice can become as calming and fulfilling as seated meditation. As a bonus end project of this pursuit of perfect can be something that you share with your loved ones and the world. But the greatest gift of all are the lessons the practice itself provides you with.

Use the *Notes* section at the end of this chapter to chart the progress in your journey. Along the way begin to pay very close attention to the quality of your actions and attention in everything you do in other areas of your life.

"Perfection is not attainable, but if we chase perfection we can catch excellence." – *Vince Lombardi*

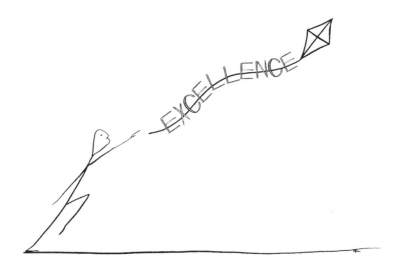

Meditation

The following simple meditation will help you to focus your full attention on a singular goal, task, or idea. It will help you to transform these things from the fragile realm of thoughts into the more tangible realm of the physical world.

1. INHALE for a count of 5 through your nose (sniff the flower). With eyes closed think of the one thing you want to become better at. Imagine yourself doing it with complete confidence, flawlessly and effortlessly;

2. HOLD the breath for a count of 5. Feel the sense of happiness, accomplishment, and satisfaction at knowing you've done your absolute best and achieved your goal;

3. EXHALE for a count of 7 through your mouth (blow out the candle). Envision that feeling of happiness, accomplishment, and satisfaction filling the space you're in and spreading to family and friends around you.

4. REPEAT for as many repetitions as you like (at least 3 are best).

Choose a single skill you'd like to become better at. Using this chapter's *Notes* section list a simple plan of action and timeline goal for mastering the one skill you choose. Over the course of the next week take steps each day to master it and record your progress.

NOTES

NOTES

NOTES

NOTES

NOTES

NOTES

NOTES

Chapter Seven

You Are What You Think

For a variety of reasons, 2020 has been a year of struggle for us all. Although it's been difficult, it's taught many of us about the importance of maintaining a proper mindset through difficult times. A few months into the pandemic I began to crave topics of conversation that were about anything other than the same old things that everyone else was discussing like: divisive political leaders; the COVID-19 pandemic; civil unrest; financial hardship; etc.

As we're all quickly learning, there is something far more dangerous than any contagion could ever hope to be. That danger is an absolute obsession with negativity. All of us are being submerged in a toxic soup of horrific stories and equally nightmarish theories of how these catastrophes have originated in mainstream and social media. To make matters worse, it seems for every story there's a counter story that is almost equally as believable. This can be so disorienting and make us feel like it's impossible to discern the truth. Being immersed in this kind of chaos and confusion for any length of time is extremely toxic and can make us feel like we've lost all control of our lives.

It's a necessity to your physical, mental, emotional, and spiritual health to find a way to take back some measure of control and cleanse yourself from all this toxicity. While you can take appropriate measures to limit the amount and sources of news you consume, it's more difficult to escape all of the other people in your life who are still addicted to these negative news outlets and social media.

Following are some strategies I've found to be a huge help to me during this pandemic. I believe these strategies could be applied during any time of hardship like: job loss, depression, times of grieving, etc.

"Life is ten percent what happens to you and ninety percent how you respond to it." – *Charles Swindoll*

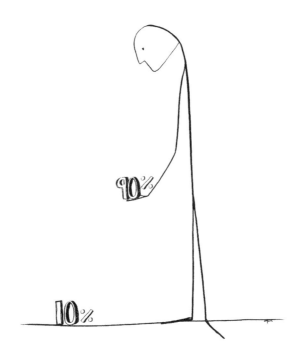

Structure

When you're immersed in a time of extreme hardship you feel disconnected, frightened, and disoriented. During these life events there's so much that's completely out of our control. How we design our daily schedules during a forced quarantine or other times of hardship like unemployment is something we still have absolutely one hundred percent control over. By purposefully designing your day you're at the same time exerting some measure of control over your life in a time where you feel helpless and this is empowering.

Wake up at a specific time every morning. Set alarms on your mobile device for certain times of the day for activities like – yoga, reading, workouts, taking virtual classes, walking the dog, and anything else you enjoy doing. Consciously fill your day with activities that fill you with a sense of positivity and purpose.

This kind of daily routine keeps your body healthy and your mind occupied. By consciously adding structure to your day you regain a measure of control that will provide less time for anxiety or depression to creep in. Always try to remember, whatever you are going through, this too shall pass.

Keeping In Touch

Socializing face-to-face is always best but when this isn't possible make it a point to use technology to keep in closer contact with family and friends, especially those who are elderly and/or more vulnerable. It could make a massive difference in the mindsets of all the parties involved. Video calls are a great alternative to face-to-face communication when in-person socializing isn't possible. Humans, even us introverts, are social beings and we need to communicate with others for our days to feel complete and fulfilled.

Thinking About Your Future

How we deal with a crisis situation, like anything else, depends on our perspective. In times of chaos we must learn to be flexible and adjust our plans to sudden life-changes that are beyond our control. We have to be ready to quickly pivot to a Plan B, Plan C, or even sometimes D.

Always try to stand up to feelings of discouragement. Instead of allowing discouragement to make you quit, try readjusting your approach and continuing to move forward, even if it's down a different path than you originally anticipated. Failure isn't a thing to be ashamed of because it's proof that you tried something worthwhile in the first place. Simply take all of the lessons you've learned from that failed attempt and try again.

Many times you'll notice something amidst the despair that can be a true gift in disguise, like the chance to start a completely different career or project. I had planned to launch a YouTube travel channel this year and my wife and I had several trips booked to begin that adventure. Of course 2020 continued on trend and travel restrictions were put into place and we had to cancel all those trips. I was feeling extremely discouraged about it but instead of giving into self-pity I decided to shift gears and used my time in forced quarantine to write this book. Now, instead of wasting countless hours moping and watching Netflix I have something more positive to show for that time.

Close your eyes and really take a moment to think about where you want to be in ten years. Using this chapter's *Notes* section write down, in precise detail, exactly where you will be living, what you will be doing, the clothes you'll be wearing, how you'll be feeling exactly one decade from today.

Next, jot down three simple things that you can do in the next year to make this vision a reality. These should be things that, in some way small or large, will make the quality of your life better than it was before. Reread what you wrote down in the *Notes* section often to help you stay focused.

All of the negative things that are happening around you and are outside of your control are only temporary and they will never define who you are. Try to use your time to reinvent a better version of yourself.

Helping Others

Nothing helps to take your mind off of the negativity surrounding you more than helping others. I've found a mobile phone app called NextDoor that allows people in the same neighborhoods to connect. One great thing people in our neighborhood are offering to do during this pandemic is running errands for those who can't make it out of their homes. This could make a huge difference in the lives of the elderly or those with mobility issues. Technology now makes helping those in need easier than ever before and it gives you a sense of satisfaction and purpose in return.

**"But I know, somehow, that only when it is dark enough
can you see the stars." – *Dr. Martin Luther King Jr.***

Meditation for Releasing Feelings of Anxiety and Inadequacy

The following simple meditation will help you to expel negative emotional states like feelings of inadequacy and anxiety. Remember, we tend to attract into our lives whatever we dwell upon. Dwell on negativity and we attract more of it into our lives. Focus on the positive and that's exactly when you will manifest into your life. Always remember the quality of your thoughts dictate the quality of your life so learn to regularly monitor your thoughts and be conscious of what is happening within your headspace. You are what you think and our thoughts are more powerful than you know.

Find a quiet, private place. Sit upright in a comfortable chair with your eyes closed and concentrate on your breath for a count of thirty.

1. INHALE for a count of 5 through your nose (sniff the flower). As you inhale imagine being filled with an intense feeling of pure joy and contentment. Breathe deeply enough that your belly expands with the inhalation. This will insure that the lower lobes of your lungs are bathed with oxygen;

2. HOLD the breath for a count of 5. As you hold your breath, concentrate fully on these feelings of joy and contentment.;

3. EXHALE for a count of 7 through your mouth (blow out the candle). Envision all feelings of despair and inadequacy exiting with your breath, like black soot from a chimney and floating away; and

4. REPEAT for as long as you like (at least 3 repetitions).

NOTES

NOTES

NOTES

NOTES

NOTES

NOTES

Chapter Eight

The Law Of Attraction

I first became familiar with the Law of Attraction from a wildly successful book first published in 2006 called, "The Secret". In the book, author Rhonda Byrne proposes that our thoughts and expectations give us much greater control of our future than most of us realize.

I read this book the year it was published and it came at a very transitional point in my life. In 2006 I was in a new relationship with my current wife, a year after a divorce. I was starting an online tea business and became much more serious about making writing less of a hobby and more of a full-time gig. This was among the handful of books that permanently changed the way I viewed the world. If you haven't read it, I highly suggest you do.

In the years that have followed I've learned through experience that the Law of Attraction is real. We have tremendous power inside of us. As explained in previous chapters, I've discovered that the quality of our thoughts, positive or negative, in large part dictate the quality of our life experience. A negative inner dialogue is the only true barrier to success and improving our lives. It's not easy to stay positive in a world where you're inundated with negativity 24/7. However, I can't stress this enough, it is absolutely crucial to train yourself to constantly monitor the quality of your thoughts and inner dialogue and shift them back to the positive realm when necessary.

"When you are joyful, when you say yes to life and have fun and project positivity all around you, you become a sun in the center of every constellation, and people want to be near you." – *Shannon Adler*

The mechanics of how your mind engages with the physical world and manifests dreams and aspirations into reality is deceptively simple. It's so simple, in fact, that you must continuously remind yourself of how it works. Our universe is an "echo chamber" that reverberates the energy we emit back to us in the form of experiences and people we cross paths with.

It's really quite remarkable when you understand how it works and begin to experiment with it. If more people knew about how effective it was, the self-help genre would cease to exist and all of the self-proclaimed gurus and life coaches would run out of customers very quickly.

Here's another reminder:

If we focus on gratitude we attract abundance into our lives.

If we allow ourselves to focus on negativity we attract struggle and despair into our lives.

That's all there is to it. Simple in theory, right?

By gratitude, I mean being sincerely grateful for all of the good things in your life. No matter how challenging your current situation is, if you think hard enough, everybody can find one thing to be grateful for. Even if all you have to be grateful for is the oxygen that's keeping you alive, acknowledge this one thing, it will be a good start.

A good example of how gratitude can radically transform something we often take for granted is the cup of coffee or tea you enjoy every day. As you're making, or buying, that warming and comforting beverage, think of all the people, knowledge, and work it took for you to enjoy that single cup.

Think about the farmer who grew the beans or the leaves and their struggles, the workers who picked the crop, the craftsmen who roasted the beans or processed the tea leaves, the many people it took to transport the product to the store you bought it from. Now think of the effort, sacrifice, the years of education and practice it took for all those people to become good at what they do.

It took the collective effort of this entire group of people just so you can have that single cup of coffee or tea. Think about this each time you have a cup of coffee or tea, pause for a moment, be grateful. The shift in perspective this exercise just gave you makes that beverage seem infinitely more delicious and special. It also makes you feel more grateful for the privilege to enjoy it, doesn't it? You can apply this same line of thought to almost anyone and anything in your life. This is living mindfully. As you begin to live more in this continuum of gratitude you will attract an immense amount of positive things into your life. You will also feel happier and more content.

"Gratitude turns what we have into enough." – Aesop

When you find one single thing to be thankful for, it will put you into a state of gratitude. A wonderful by-product of entering into a state of gratitude is that you will develop an appreciation for what you have and the restlessness of constant yearning for more and better things will begin to dissipate. As Aesop said, "Gratitude turns what we have into enough."

Once you're in that state of gratitude it will lead you down the path of discovering more and more until it causes a chain reaction that eventually changes your life.

Becoming A Conduit For Abundance

Switching your consciousness into a state of gratitude is how you transform yourself into a conduit for abundance. It may sound like woo-woo, new-age mumbo jumbo but don't knock it until you try it. This tool will be especially useful during these challenging times.

Be aware that abundance won't just be magically dropped into your lap. You must: 1) have and hold a clear vision of what you want; and 2) be willing to do the physical work to achieve your goal(s) as well.

What you will quickly learn from residing in this state of gratitude is that it's a tool. This tool will attract certain people and situations into your life that will create an environment that makes your goals easier to achieve. This is called synchronicity and it's so important that I dedicated an entire chapter to it in my first meditation book, The Perfect Pause.

Maya Angelou was quoted as saying, "Ask for what you want and be prepared to get it." I believe this to be true. Always hold the belief that the future is limitless and the universe can deliver almost anything you wish, when you truly believe that your inner thoughts start to become your outer reality.

Using Tech For Wellness

Once more, the quality of your thoughts determine the quality of our entire life experience. Remind yourself frequently how important this is. Most of us have mobile devices that we check hundreds of times per day and never leave our sides. Did you know this tech can be used as a valuable tool for our personal development?

Set a recurring reminder on your phone to notify you once (or twice) a day with a message, *"What Are You Grateful For?"* This will remind you to shift back into a state of gratitude if you've allowed yourself to be distracted and/or derailed.

Meditation For Attracting Abundance

Find a quiet place that will be free from distractions. Sit upright in a comfortable chair with your eyes closed and concentrate on your breath for a count of thirty...to breathe properly for meditation just remember, "sniff the flower" (inhale), "blow out the candle" (exhale).

Think about a situation you've experienced in the past where you've felt extremely grateful. This could be anything: a long wished-for gift you've received;

money you've found when you've truly needed it; traveling to a destination you've always wanted to experience; or eating or drinking after a period of great hunger or thirst.

1. INHALE for a count of 5 through your nose (sniff the flower). Breathe in the feeling of joy that the memory of this deep sense of gratitude sparks. Inhale deeply enough that your belly expands with the inhalation. This will insure that the lower lobes of your lungs are bathed with oxygen;

2. HOLD the breath for a count of 5. Concentrate on the feeling of pure joy and gratitude. Feel it growing in intensity and coursing throughout your body;

3. EXHALE for a count of 7 through your mouth (blow out the candle). As you breathe out imagine the space you're currently in filling up with positive energy and abundance.

4. REPEAT for as long as you like (at least 3 repetitions).

After you practice this very simple meditation technique it's helpful to linger in the serenity for a few minutes — focus on your happiness, health, and overall well-being.

Over the course of the next week jot down at least one thing per day you're grateful for in the *Notes* section at the end of this chapter. It's also helpful to write a few words about how this thing you're grateful for makes you feel.

NOTES

NOTES

NOTES

NOTES

NOTES

NOTES

Chapter Nine

Stop Giving Your Power Away

Choosing the path that allows you to become the absolute best version of yourself isn't always easy in the short term, but in the long run it rewards you with huge dividends. When you begin to realize how profoundly your everyday actions influence those people around you (and vice versa) it can begin to seem more like a moral obligation to be as smart, self-aware, and compassionate as you're capable of.

You may not realize it but each one of us has great power. Each time you interact with someone you leave them with a subset of residual feelings. These feelings have the power to change the emotional state of that person. This interaction can be as complex as an hours-long conversation or as simple as a five second interaction with a cashier at a gas station.

A very useful question to ask yourself every single day is:

Are you leaving the people you interact with in a better or a worse state than before they met you?

For example, think about that last innocent mistake you made while behind the wheel in traffic. It could have been cutting someone else off who was in your blindspot, failing to use a turn signal, etc. We've all made those absentminded mistakes that have sparked a fit of road rage from another driver. Although you didn't mean to cut them off (or whatever else it was you did) their beeping, yelling, and/or cursing probably ruined part of your day.

To make matters worse, this road rager's temper tantrum will even start a chain reaction, if you let it. You may decide to retaliate, escalating the situation further. Even if you don't retaliate in that moment you may hold onto the negative experience and it might make you treat someone else badly at a later point in the day. Not only is this horrible for your own emotional and physical health but it has the potential to be bad for everyone else you come in contact with afterwards. It's much better to break the cycle.

The important thing to remember is we have a choice as to how we react to these kinds of situations. A majority of people have been conditioned to believe they're being strong by retaliating against someone who says or does something rude to them but it's quite the opposite.

Each time we choose the path of retaliation to this kind of impulsive behavior we perpetuate a chain reaction of negativity. In losing our temper and retaliating we also unwillingly give our power away to someone else.

How could this be possible? By allowing complete strangers the ability to change our mental and emotional state with just a few words, a gesture, or an action we're allowing them to hack our emotions and manipulate us. In just a few seconds this kind of manipulation can escalate into a dangerous situation that has enormous consequences. Most miserable people enjoy nothing more than spreading their misery. Truly strong people keep their power and simply don't allow their emotions to be this easily manipulated.

"You have power over your mind – not outside events. Realize this, and you will find strength." – *Marcus Aurelius*

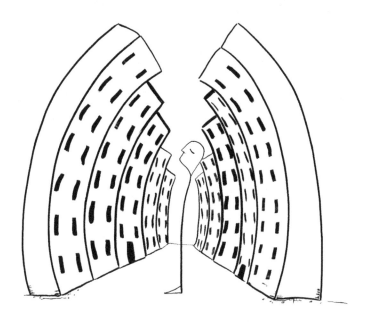

One of the amazing side-effects of meditation is it allows us to become more introspective instead of just impulsively reacting to what unfolds in our environment. It's a lot like installing virus protection software in your brain that offers us a layer of protection from these "hackers" who are trying to manipulate us for their own goals or amusement.

Meditation also provides us with another very valuable feature, a pause button. Once you become mindful, through the practice of meditation, you tend to not instinctively react to situations based on emotion. Instead you give yourself the cushion of a few seconds to analyze a situation before deciding how you're going to react. It's very important to remember that sometimes a few seconds can make the difference between going about your day peacefully or reacting to a situation in a way that could alter the course of your entire life.

"He who controls others may be powerful but he who has mastered himself is mightier still." – *Lao Tzu*

Once you begin to see the world from this introspective angle you will see that a lot of things start to look different. Becoming conscious of your reactions will make you feel as though a thick fog has lifted, you'll be able to see both yourself and the world around you in a more honest light.

You'll start to recognize your own deficiencies and weaknesses. By recognizing them you'll be able to begin to actively work to overcome them. This will allow you to reclaim your personal power and this will set you on a path of self-directed evolution that will change your life more than you could possibly imagine.

This is how we change the world for the better, one person at a time. Making a promise to yourself to be a better person tomorrow than you are today is the best gift you can give to the world. It all begins with you.

Meditation

Find a quiet place that will be free from distractions. Sit upright in a comfortable chair with your eyes closed and concentrate on your breath for a count of thirty. Then:

1. INHALE through your nose for a count of five (*sniff the flower*). While inhaling, imagine all of the anger you're holding inside of you being extracted from the furthest reaches of your body and mind;

2. HOLD the breath for a count of 5 (*pause*). Imagine the anger all gathering in your lungs; and

3. EXHALE from your mouth for a count of 7 (*blow out the candle*). Release all of the anger and envision it floating away, like a helium-filled balloon, into the sky.

4. REPEAT for as long as you like (at least 3 repetitions).

Now think about a situation you've experienced in the past where you've lost your temper and greatly regret it. Revisit that memory, with closed eyes. Imagine yourself reacting in a different and more positive way. Think about how much better of an outcome you would have experienced.

With closed eyes repeat the following affirmations three times each.

I will not give my power away.
I will not give my power away.
I will not give my power away.

I have the power to change my destiny.
I have the power to change my destiny.
I have the power to change my destiny.

I choose positivity over negativity, peace over chaos.
I choose positivity over negativity, peace over chaos.
I choose positivity over negativity, peace over chaos.

Using the following *Notes* section think about things that regularly trigger anger inside of you. Now list circumstances in which you habitually lose your temper and how it makes you feel afterwards. Practice the meditation and affirmations in this chapter for a week then reread what you wrote. Think about how you can permanently change your pattern of behavior to experience better results and retain more of your personal power.

NOTES

NOTES

NOTES

NOTES

NOTES

NOTES

Chapter Ten

Negative Feelings, A Roadmap
To Self-Improvement

We live in very trying times there's plenty to be angry about. Even though anger and hate are destructive, people have become addicted to these negative emotions and are drawn back to it again and again, like a potent drug. Unless you're willing to completely retreat from society and become a hermit there's no way to fully shield yourself from negativity.

Feelings of anger and hate can teach us something if we're willing to think about why the emotions are being triggered inside of us. These destructive feelings can even provide a roadmap to us for our own self-improvement. We must learn to not only manage these feelings but also learn to listen to what these feelings of negativity are trying to tell us about ourselves. *Why do we hate what we hate?* It's imperative to our own well-being that we figure this out.

Science has proven that negative emotions like hate, if left unchecked and unprocessed, are like poison to both the mental and physical health of the person who holds onto them. Holding onto anger and hate for any length of time can lead to a multitude of mental and medical problems like depression, anxiety, high blood pressure, coronary artery disease, and even cancer. We must learn to master these negative emotions and release them or they will master us by stealing away our personal power, life balance, and decimating our inner peace.

How can we successfully manage our negative feelings?

1. We can take the reactive approach and attempt to quell anger that already exists inside of us through regular meditation; or

2. We can take it a step further and try to get to the root cause of why certain behaviors and situations trigger our negative emotions to begin with.

I recommend a combination of both #1 and #2. I'll expound on this more in the exercise below.

"Everything that irritates us about others can lead us to an understanding about ourselves." – *Carl Jung*

Mindfulness Exercise

Take a few moments to think of a person in recent days that has annoyed you in some way, even the example seems vague or insignificant. What exact traits and behaviors in that person angered or annoyed you? Now think about whether or not you yourself exhibit the same behavior that you're despising in the other person. Is there a time when you behaved in the same way or did the same thing yourself?

For a variety of reasons we often become blind to certain aspects of our own behavior. The funny thing about the human psyche is we unconsciously recognize our own flaws and deficiencies in other people and we often become angry and/or hate them for it.

When we experience hate or anger the source or trigger of these *negative emotions often represent everything WE WISH WE WEREN'T.* For example, if we routinely notice narcissistic tendencies in others and are deeply troubled by this it's important to have a moment of self-reflection and dig deep to determine if we can identify this trait inside of ourselves. If the answer is yes, we can promptly get to work on correcting the behavior. Whenever we feel anger or hate towards anything it's very important to do an honest self-audit. Sometimes the search will come up empty but it can be surprising how often it doesn't. Identifying, admitting to, and overcoming our own flaws can be difficult work. However, in many cases, we will find the doors to success, true happiness, and abundance in our own lives are locked until we have the courage to do this work.

Pause a moment to let that sink in and in time you'll realize how much truth there is in it.

Also, when we feel envy or jealousy the trigger of *these emotions represent things that WE WISH WE WERE or things WE WISH WE HAD.* For example, if we know someone who seems to float through life care-free as we go about our days feeling anxious or worried it's easy to be envious of that person. Additionally, if someone your own age has achieved a much higher level of success in their career or relationships sometimes our first instinct is to feel jealous. Competitiveness, the tendency to compare ourselves to others, is deeply embedded in our human DNA. It's easy to succumb to our envy and jealousy of others and become engulfed in drama and gossip about them. This doesn't benefit us one bit and leaves us right back where we started or worse. It's more difficult, but infinitely more productive, to think about ways in which we can improve the areas of our own life that are triggering our feelings of insecurity. If we do the latter, even negative emotions like envy and jealousy can be valuable tools in our self-evolution.

"Negative emotions often represent everything we wish we weren't."

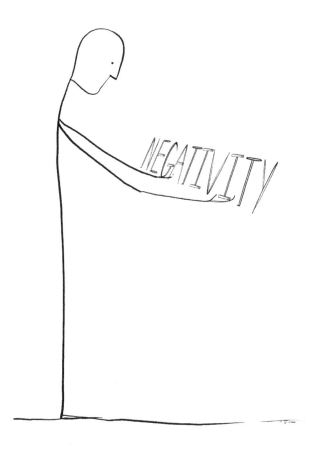

Ego, Friend or Foe?

At first your ego will try to create a smokescreen by manifesting a plethora of excuses and denial. Your ego is a great deceiver and probably the largest road-block to your own self-improvement. However, if you sift through the excuses the truth will become more clear. With patience and courage to face the truth, we can begin to work on improving these negative aspects of ourselves.

Again, when you experience anger/hate the steps are:

1. Focus on the negative emotion. Pinpoint the exact behavior in others that triggers feelings of anger/hate;

2. Identify that behavior in yourself. *In what ways do you sometimes exhibit the same behavior?* Think of a precise example; and

3. Work on self-improvement. Make it a mission to try to fix these aspects of yourself. By doing so you'll kill the anger/hate at its very roots.

Now repeat this process with every negative emotion you feel. Of course, this won't eliminate all instances of negative emotion, sometimes people are just difficult, but it will get rid of a lot of them and will give you a much greater understanding of yourself in the process.

Meditation

If you discover the feelings of negativity aren't rooted in yourself the following meditation/affirmation is a great way to eliminate the poison of negativity and prevent damage to your mental and physical health.

Find a quiet place that will be free from distractions. Sit upright in a comfortable chair with your eyes closed and concentrate on your breath for a count of thirty...to breathe properly for meditation just remember,

1. INHALE through your nose for a count of 5 (sniff the flower), as you breathe in imagine positive energy and bright white light filling up your body;

2. HOLD the breath for a count of 5 (pause), feel the positive energy coursing through your being and scrubbing away all the hate and anger you hold inside;

3. EXHALE from your mouth for a count of 7 (blow out the candle), as you breathe out feel the hate and anger escaping through your breath.

4. REPEAT for as long as you like (at least 3 repetitions).

Affirmation

Repeat the following lines:

Whisper words of sadness, release them from your soul.

Watch each sorrow take its flight, feel what it is to be whole.

Embrace the calm, revel in peace, absence of pain, all worries cease.

You deserve every happiness, you deserve to be free.

Whisper these words in perfect peace and you will forever after be.

After you recite the lines of this poem, linger in the feelings of serenity for a few minutes. Focus entirely on the peace you feel and ways in which you can improve your own behavior and become a better version of yourself each day.

Practice this meditation and affirmation once a day for a week. After each meditation/affirmation session, using the *Notes* section at the end of this chapter, list traits, behaviors, or other things that trigger feelings of anger and hate inside yourself towards others. Dig deep inside of yourself and explore and identify how some of those things that are regularly triggering your negative emotions also dwell inside of you. Think about ways you can change yourself to eliminate these triggers.

NOTES

NOTES

NOTES

NOTES

NOTES

NOTES

Then Our Peace Will Come

How will we
find our way back
to the middle of the road?

Let the old folks
show their scars of sacrifice
and tell the stories the photos
on their walls recall.

Stop pretending.
Stop expecting.
Stop hiding
our collective sins.
Stop believing
politicians' lies.

The world they sell us
is black and white
but, in truth,
it is billions of
beautiful shades of grey,
stop hating for a moment...
please JUST STOP.

All of us are hurting.

Breathe in, think,
open your heart,
open your mind,
relish this life, breathe out,
then our Peace will come.

Start discussing.

Start forgiving.
Start being kind.
Start realizing
more than one version
of the truth can exist.

Start agreeing to disagree.
Start allowing people
to have their dignities.
Start practicing love
or we'll all die twisted by hate,
this doesn't have to be our fate,
JUST START.

Then our Peace will come.

When together we relish in
our collective self-worth...
the laughter of our children,
the smell of sweet sage and Earth,
the pine trees after the rain.
When we train our eyes
to see beyond our pain,
this is when the bars
will come into focus,
we will finally see the prison cell
we are all held in
and, together, figure out
how to make a break,
for goodness sake, start today,
then our Peace will come.

One Final Note

I've traveled extensively over the past few years and have gotten into the habit of bringing copies of my first meditation book, *The Perfect Pause*, with me. I give them away to people I cross paths with, when inspiration strikes. I also leave signed copies in Airbnbs my wife and I stay in during our travels. I always hope the right person finds them and it helps them in some way. So if you've found the book when you're vacationing in Amsterdam, London, or Montreal I've likely stayed in those Airbnbs. I plan on doing the very same thing with this book.

For the past couple of years I've been contemplating the sequel to my first meditation book, *The Perfect Pause*. The ideas presented in this book have bubbled up organically over the last year in the form of blog posts on the blogging platform Hive (snap QR Code below to visit my blog). After working on that mindfulness series it dawned on me that a book about mindfulness is the logical sequel. Learning to live in a constant flow-state of mindfulness is the perfect way to put the many benefits earned from a daily meditation practice into use in this physical world.

Thank you so much for reading this book. I hope it makes a difference in your life.

Previously Published Books

Please visit Eric's website and Amazon page to learn more about his previous published books including his first book on meditation, *The Perfect Pause: Meditating Your Way To The Ultimate You.*

Also available is his sci-fi novel, *Alarm Clock Dawn,* which was the first full-length, serialized, novel to be published on a blockchain in 2016.

Eric's Blog

For a daily dose of Eric's writing please visit his blog on the Hive platform.

Do you have something to say or share with the world? If the answer is yes, please consider joining our growing global community on Hive. Instead of your data being sold as it is on other mainstream social media platforms, with Hive you have the potential to earn cryptocurrency every time you create content and/ or comment or vote on other users' content. On Hive you aren't the product, your content is. Snap QR Code below to join Hive and start blogging today.

Made in the USA
Monee, IL
10 December 2020